Contents

Where is China? 4

Meet Liu Jiasi 6

At school 8

Having fun 10

City and country 12

Meet Tao Kui 14

Daily life 16

Playtime 18

Art, music and theatre 20

Meet Thomas 22

Having fun 24

School and play 26

China's history 28

Chinese fact file 30

Glossary 31

More books to read 31

Index 32

Words appearing in the text in bold, **like this**, are explained in the Glossary.

 Find out more about China at
www.heinemannexplore.co.uk

Where is china?

To learn more about China we meet three children who live there. China is in Asia. China is the fourth largest country in the world.

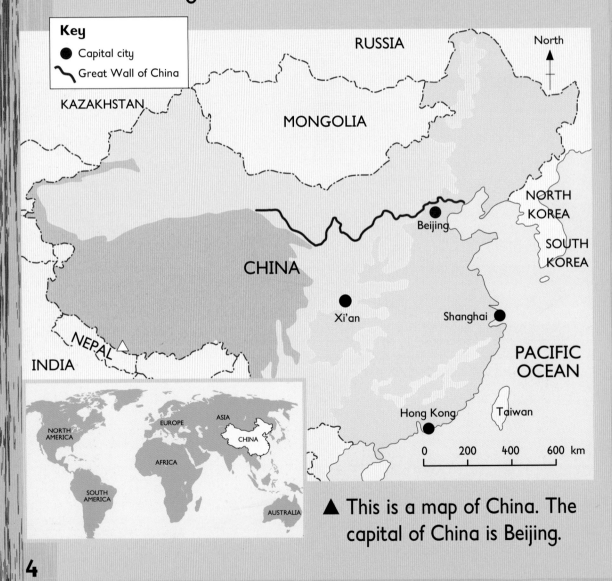

Key
- ● Capital city
- ∿ Great Wall of China

RUSSIA

North

KAZAKHSTAN

MONGOLIA

NORTH KOREA

Beijing

SOUTH KOREA

CHINA

NEPAL

INDIA

Xi'an

Shanghai

PACIFIC OCEAN

Hong Kong

Taiwan

0   200   400   600 km

NORTH AMERICA

EUROPE

ASIA

CHINA

AFRICA

SOUTH AMERICA

AUSTRALIA

▲ This is a map of China. The capital of China is Beijing.

We're from

China

Emma Lynch

H **www.heinemann.co.uk/library**
Visit our website to find out more information about **Heinemann Library** books.

To order:
☎ Phone 44 (0) 1865 888066
🖹 Send a fax to 44 (0) 1865 314091
🖥 Visit the Heinemann Bookshop at www.heinemann.co.uk/library to browse our catalogue and order online.

First published in Great Britain by Heinemann Library, Halley Court, Jordan Hill, Oxford OX2 8EJ, part of Harcourt Education.
Heinemann is a registered trademark of Harcourt Education Ltd.

Editorial: Jilly Attwood and Kate Bellamy
Design: Ron Kamen and Celia Jones
Photographer: Debbie Rowe
Picture Research: Maria Joannou and Erica Newbery
Production: Séverine Ribierre

Originated by Ambassador Litho Ltd

Printed and bound in China by South China Printing Company

10 digit ISBN 0 431 11946 5 (hardback)
13 digit ISBN 978 0 431 11946 5 (hardback)
09 08 07 06 05
10 9 8 7 6 5 4 3 2 1

10 digit ISBN 0 431 11953 8 (paperback)
13 digit ISBN 978 0 431 11953 3 (paperback)
10 09 08 07 06
10 9 8 7 6 5 4 3 2 1

British Library Cataloguing in Publication Data

Lynch, Emma
  We're From China
  951'.06

A full catalogue record for this book is available from the British Library.

Acknowledgements
Corbis p. **30c** (royalty free); Harcourt Education pp. **1, 5a, 5b, 6a, 6b, 7, 8a, 8b, 9a, 9b, 10a, 10b, 11, 12a, 12b, 13, 14a, 14b, 15a, 15b, 16a, 16b, 17a, 17b, 18, 19a, 19b, 20, 21a, 21b, 22a, 22b, 23a, 23b, 24, 25, 26a, 26b, 27, 28a, 28b, 29, 30a, 30b** (Debbie Rowe).

Cover photograph of Liu Jiasi and classmates, reproduced with permission of Harcourt Education/Debbie Rowe.

Many thanks to Liu Jiasi, Tao Kui, Thomas and their families.

Every effort has been made to contact copyright holders of any material reproduced in this book. Any omissions will be rectified in subsequent printings if notice is given to the publishers.

The paper used to print this book comes from sustainable resources.

North China is very cold. South China is very warm. China has many mountains. Most people live in the east of China, where the land is lower.

More people live in China ▶ than any other country of the world.

▲ China has mountains and hills, grasslands and **deserts**.

Meet Liu Jiasi

Liu Jiasi is six years old. She lives in a flat in Beijing with her mother and father. Liu Jiasi's parents work at the university in Beijing.

Liu Jiasi's father

Liu Jiasi's mother

Liu Jiasi

▲ Liu Jiasi's favourite food is tomato and egg soup.

In the evenings the family eat together. Liu Jiasi's mother cooks. Sometimes they go out to eat.

At school

Liu Jiasi goes to school five days a week. She lives near her school, so she walks there. She has lessons in Chinese, physical education, science, maths and painting.

▼ There are 40 children in Liu Jiasi's class. Her best friend is called Liu Jing.

Liu Jiasi likes painting, science and maths. She wants to be a scientist when she grows up. Liu Jiasi does not like physical education.

▼ Liu Jiasi's school do physical education outside in lines.

Having fun

At home, Liu Jiasi likes to play with her toys and draw. She also enjoys riding her bike. Sometimes she and her parents visit the park.

▼ Liu Jiasi enjoys trips out in Beijing.

Liu Jiasi looks forward to the New Year celebrations. At New Year, families give their children presents of money in red envelopes. These envelopes are called **hong bao**.

City and country

Cities like Beijing are big and full of people. There are lots of taxis, buses and lorries. People go to work in offices and visit shops.

Life in town is ▶ noisy and busy.

The countryside is much quieter. There are not many cars or lorries. Families live together or very near each other in villages.

In the country, people ▶ work on the land and grow their own food.

Meet Tao Kui

Tao Kui is seven years old. He lives in a house in a farming village. His parents are farmers. They grow rice, **water chestnuts** and **squash**.

Tao Kui's mother

Tao Kui's grandfather

Tao Kui's grandmother

Tao Kui's father

Tao Kui

▲ Tao Kui lives with his mother, father and grandparents.

Tao Kui would ▶
like to be a
farmer, like
his father.

Tao Kui's aunts and uncles also live in the village. He visits them often. He likes to play outside because there is so much space.

Daily life

Tao Kui goes to school. He also helps the family with their work. He walks the water buffaloes to the water, so they don't get too hot.

◄ Sometimes Tao Kui goes swimming too!

chopsticks

▲ Tao Kui's family use **chopsticks** to eat their food.

The family grows a lot of the food they eat. They buy the rest of their food from the market. Tao Kui likes eating fish but he does not like spicy food.

Playtime

Tao Kui has a new puppy to play with. He also has lots of friends who live nearby. They play outside all the time because it is very hot.

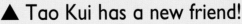

▲ Tao Kui has a new friend!

Tao Kui and his friends like to climb
trees, go swimming and ride their
bikes. They have to be careful because
there are lots of snakes in the area.

Art, music and theatre

China is famous for making pictures of plants and animals on pottery, paper and silk. Another art is to paint Chinese signs on special paper or silk. This is called **calligraphy**.

▲ This boy is learning to do calligraphy.

▼ Chinese opera is a mixture
of singing, acting, acrobatics
and music.

Lots of Chinese people enjoy theatre,
music and dance. There are many art
festivals. Many Chinese people like
Chinese opera too.

Meet Thomas

Thomas is eight years old. He lives in a flat in Hong Kong. Thomas' parents are out at work all day. When Thomas finishes school, a maid looks after him.

Thomas's mother

Thomas's grandmothers

Thomas's father

Thomas

▲ Thomas lives with his mother, father and their maid.

▲ Some people do **tai chi** in the garden by the flats.

Lots of people live in the same block of flats as Thomas' family. His family share a garden with the other people who live in their block of flats.

Having fun

Thomas has lots of fun after school. He likes reading, playing with building bricks and doing **tae kwon do**.

▲ Thomas is dressed for tae kwon do.

▼ Sometimes Thomas and his parents go on boat trips to the islands near Hong Kong.

Thomas also enjoys days out with his parents. They visit the park or the beach. They have barbecues and visit museums. They have even been on a helicopter tour!

School and play

Thomas goes to school every day on the bus. He has lots of friends at school. His best friend is Tommy Lam, who is very clever.

▼ Thomas wears a school uniform.

After school, Thomas and his friends
play at the playground. They wear
play clothes like shorts and T-shirts.
Thomas wears new clothes for the
Chinese New Year celebrations.

China's history

China has a very long and important history. This pottery army of soldiers and horses is in a museum at Xi'an. The army is over 2000 years old.

◀ Every soldier has been made to look slightly different.

▼ Many tourists visit the Great
Wall of China every year.

The Great Wall of China was built
more than 2000 years ago. It was built
to keep China's enemies out. It is so
long it can even be seen from space!

Chinese fact file

Flag **Capital city** **Money**

Beijing

Yuan

Religion
• Most people in China do not follow a religion, but a small number of people are Taoist, Buddhist, Muslim or Christian.

Language
• There are many languages and dialects in China. People might speak Standard Chinese or Mandarin, Cantonese or Shanghaiese.

Try speaking Mandarin!
ni hao... Hello.
wo jiao... My name is…
xie xie... Thank you.

 Find out more about China at
www.heinemannexplore.co.uk

Glossary

calligraphy beautiful handwriting done with a special pen or brush

chopsticks two special sticks used to eat food with instead of knives and forks. They are held in one hand.

desert very hot, dry area of land that has almost no rain and very few plants

festival big celebration for a town or country

hong bao means 'red packet' in Chinese

squash vegetable similar to a marrow

Tai Chi gentle movements and breathing exercises to help people feel calm

Tae Kwon Do sport that uses balancing and kicking skills

university where people go to continue learning when they finish school

water chestnut fruit from a plant that grows in water. It tastes a bit like a nut.

More books to read

Traditional Tales from China, Vic Parker, Philip Ardagh, Michael Fisher, (Belitha Press, 2001)

C is for China, Sungwan So (Frances Lincoln Ltd, 2000)

World of Festivals: Chinese New Year, Catherine Chambers, (Evans Brothers, 1999)

Index

Chinese New Year 11, 27

city 6, 12

family 6, 7, 10, 11, 13, 14, 15, 16, 17, 22, 23, 25

food 7, 13, 14, 17

Great Wall of China 29

homes 6, 13, 14, 22, 23

job 6, 9, 12, 13, 14, 15, 16, 22

school 8, 9, 16, 22, 24, 26

trips 10, 25

village 13, 14, 15